WE BOTH READ

Parent's Intro

We Both Read is the first s
invite parents and children to s
by taking turns reading aloud. T
vation, which was developed
reading specialists, invites parents to read the more sop
ticated text on the left-hand pages, while children are
encouraged to read the right-hand pages, which have been
written at one of three early reading levels.

Reading aloud is one of the most important activities
parents can share with their child to assist their reading
development. However, We Both Read goes beyond reading *to* a child and allows parents to share reading *with* a
child. We Both Read is so powerful and effective because it
combines two key elements in learning: "showing" (the
parent reads) and "doing" (the child reads). The result is not
only faster reading development for the child, but a much
more enjoyable and enriching experience for both!

Most of the words used in the child's text should be
familiar to them. Others can easily be sounded out. An occa-
sional difficult word will be first introduced in the parent's
text, distinguished with **bold lettering**. Pointing out these
words, as you read them, will help familiarize them to your
child. You may also find it helpful to read the entire book
aloud yourself the first time, then invite your child to par-
ticipate on the second reading. Also note that the parent's
text is preceded by a "talking parent" icon: ⊚ ; and the
child's text is preceded by a "talking child" icon: ⊚ .

We Both Read books is a fun, easy way to encourage
and help your child to read — and a wonderful way to start
your child off on a lifetime of reading enjoyment!

We Both Read: Being Safe

We Both Read® is a trademark of Treasure Bay, Inc.

Published by Treasure Bay, Inc.
17 Parkgrove Drive
South San Francisco, CA 94080 USA

PRINTED IN SINGAPORE

Library of Congress Catalog Card Number: 2002094716

Hardcover ISBN: 1-891327-51-8
Paperback ISBN: 1-891327-52-6

FIRST EDITION

We Both Read® Books
Patent No. 5,957,693

Visit us online at:
www.webothread.com

Being Safe

Note to Parents and Teachers

This book presents many important ideas and issues about child safety. While the book can be read in one sitting, you might also want to consider sharing the reading one chapter at a time. You and your young reader can then talk about the ideas presented in each chapter, and talk about related safety issues, before continuing with the book.

Table of Contents

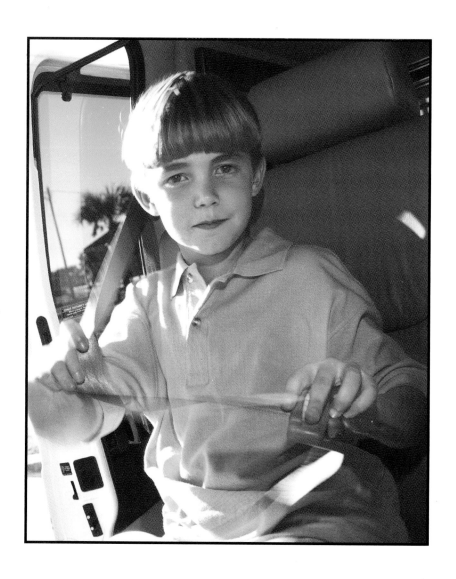

CHAPTER 1

Introduction

Always wear a seat belt when riding in a car. Use the crosswalk when crossing the street. Be sure to wear a helmet when you use your bike, skates, or scooter. These are just a few **ideas** to start you on your way to being safe.

 This book is filled with **ideas** on how to be safe. You may already know some of the ideas. You may learn some new ideas too.

   There are many different **safety** tips presented in this book. Be sure to discuss all these suggestions with your parents to be sure that they are right for you.

Your parents may have some other ideas for you about **safety**. Parents can be pretty smart sometimes!

CHAPTER 2

Safety at Home

One of the biggest safety hazards in the home is accidental poisoning. Many things are poisonous and some are hard to spot. Medicine can look like candy. Household cleaners can look like soft drinks. Always ask your parents or an adult you know before eating or drinking anything that you are not sure about.

Yew branch with berry (poisonous)

   Some plants can make you very sick if you eat them. Don't put anything in your mouth until you know that it's safe.

   **Accidents** happen. You might cut your hand on broken glass. You could burn yourself on a hot pot. If an accident happens to you or a friend, try to stay calm. Go to the nearest trusted adult and ask for help.

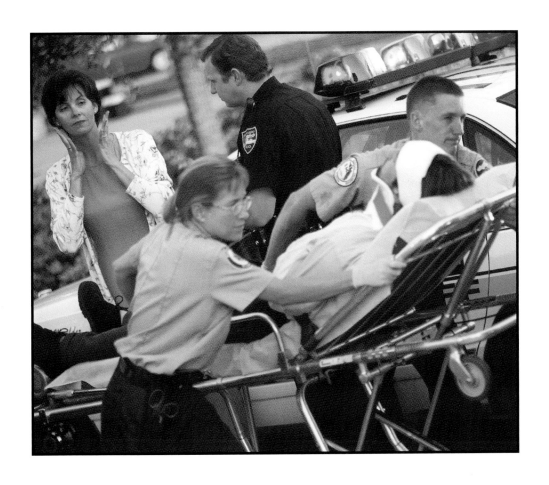

Adults have **accidents** too. If you or an adult need help, you can call 9-1-1.

Fire safety should be practiced by everyone. Here are a few simple rules to **remember**:

- Don't play with matches or lighters.
- Don't use the stove without adult supervision.
- Be extra careful around heaters and open fires.
- Make sure your home is equipped with smoke detectors.

If your clothes catch on fire, do not run!

Stop where you are.

Drop to the ground and roll.

Remember, "STOP, DROP, AND ROLL."

 Work together with your family to make an escape plan in case of a fire in your home. Every room should have two ways out. One way out could be a door and the other could be a window.

Plan a meeting place outside. Everyone should go there once they are out of the house.

CHAPTER 3

Safety at School

Walking to school can be fun and safe when you follow a few simple rules:
- Walk with a friend or a group of friends.
- Cross the street at a light whenever possible.
- Use crosswalks where no light is available.

Many kids ride to school in a car. Be sure to wear your seat belt or sit in a car seat every time you ride in a car.

   It's possible that someone you don't know may offer you a ride. They may tell you that it's okay with your mom or that your dad has asked them to pick you up. Do not get in the car with this person and tell a trusted adult about him or her as soon as possible.

 Never get in a car with someone you don't know. Don't even go near the car to talk to them. That's the best way to stay safe!

A bus takes some kids to school every morning. Sometimes a bus takes a class on a field trip. Whenever you are on a bus it's important to stay in your seat, talk quietly, and **obey** the rules of the bus driver.

You might ride your bike to school. A safe bike rider **obeys** the rules of the road.

Teachers have rules that you must follow while you are at school. Some rules are for the classroom and some are for recess. Many of these rules are there for your safety.

Most schools have fire drills. They teach you what to do if there is a fire at your school.

CHAPTER 4

Safety at Play

There are many ways to play outdoors. You can skate, swim, play sports, or swing on the monkey bars. However you like to play, be sure to play safely. Wear the proper equipment and don't try to show-off by taking unnecessary chances.

   Helmets help keep your head from getting
hurt. Use a helmet every time you skate or ride
your bike or scooter.

Water play is lots of fun, but it can also be dangerous. Keep your water play safe by following these rules:

- Always wear a life jacket when in a boat or if you don't know how to swim.
- Be sure there is adult supervision before going into the water.
- Learn how to swim.
- Swim with a buddy.

 You should always *walk* when you are near water. Running could make you slip and fall.

 Playgrounds and parks are great places to run and laugh and have a good time with friends. To be safe, never go to a park by yourself. Be sure an adult knows where you are and ask permission before going somewhere else.

 Stay with your friends. Take someone with you when you go to use the bathroom.

Be sure to tell a trusted adult immediately if someone you don't know tries to talk to you or asks for your help. No adult should be asking a child for help. They should be asking another adult.

   A person might seem to be very nice. He might want to buy you ice cream. But you should never go anywhere with someone you don't know.

 Dogs and puppies are cute, but they might not be safe. Even a friendly dog may bite if he gets scared or excited. Be sure to ask the owner if it's okay before you approach a strange dog.

If the dog doesn't have an owner, stay away.
Tell an adult right away if a dog bites you!

 Do you know what to do if you find a gun or a knife in the grass? How about an old firecracker or a hypodermic needle? Or a bag filled with something that you've never seen before?

Don't pick it up! Tell an adult right away.
It's better to be safe than sorry.

CHAPTER 5

Things You Should Know

 Work with your parents to **learn** your name, address, and telephone number. Only give this information out to a police officer or other adult that you trust.

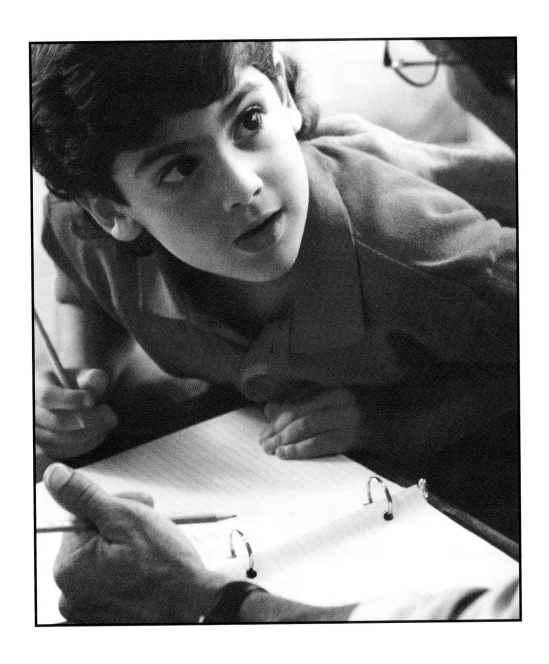

 Learn the full name of your parents. You should know their first name and their last name.

If anyone treats you in a way that makes you feel uncomfortable or scared, you have a right to tell them to stop. It is important to tell a trusted adult if something like this ever happens to you.

 Tell an adult if another child says he's going to hurt you. No one has the right to hurt you in any way.

   It's important to know when and how to dial 9-1-1.
Never dial 9-1-1 unless there is a REAL EMERGENCY—
not even to practice! An emergency is any situation where
someone has suddenly become seriously sick, badly hurt,
or is in real danger. If an adult cannot call 9-1-1 and there
is a real emergency, you can call.

    Stay calm when the 9-1-1 person answers. Tell them
what your emergency is.

   Give them your name and address.
Stay on the phone with them until they
tell you to hang up.

   Now you know all kinds of things about being safe!
You've learned how to avoid some bad situations by taking
preventive measures and you've learned how to handle
things in case a bad situation should occur.

Talk with your parents about other ways to be safe. Being safe is easy when you know the right thing to do!

If you liked **Being Safe** here are two other
We Both Read® Books you are sure to enjoy!

Written with the advice of Dr. Ronald Bachman,
M.D., this book explains how doing simple things
can help to keep us healthy. The book shows how
everyday play activities can provide the exercise we
need and how important it is to eat nutritious foods,
drink water and get enough sleep. It also covers easy
ways to help prevent spreading germs and how health
care professionals can help us to stay healthy.